W9-CQX-718

This guide covers the legal and ethics issues that arise most frequently in practice. The contents of the guide are intended for general information and should not be construed as legal advice or legal opinion. A reader with a specific legal question should consult an attorney since jurisdictional laws governing the issues here vary considerably.

This guide, or any portion of it, may not be reproduced without the written consent of the American Association for Marriage and Family Therapy.

© 2016 by the American Association for Marriage and Family Therapy

TABLE OF CONTENTS

PART I:
THE THERAPIST
AND THE OFFICE

Chapter 1: Getting Started in Private Practice

Once your license is finally issued, you may choose to work in an agency setting, or you may want to start your own private practice. For many, private practice is a goal they have been seeking from the beginning of their pursuit of the license.

Private practice allows therapists to set their own fees, determine their hours of practice, select the location where they practice, vacation when they want, and decide how small or big their enterprise will be. In essence, private practice allows licensees to be in charge of their own businesses. It is important for a therapist to consider some legal and business issues when starting or conducting a private practice. This chapter explores some of the basic issues. Since the laws and regulations of each jurisdiction vary, it is important to obtain legal or other consultation before action is taken.

FORM OF DOING BUSINESS/FICTITIOUS NAMES

The most common form of doing business for marriage and family therapists in private practice is the sole proprietorship. This simply means that you are the sole owner of the business. Thus, the name of the typical practice would be Alice Z. Jones, Licensed Marriage and Family Therapist. Usually, there are no forms to file or documents to execute in order to form a sole proprietorship. Therapists conducting business in this form simply find an office, get business cards and stationery printed, and begin operation. In many jurisdictions (e.g., cities, counties, villages, townships), sole proprietors and others (partnerships, corporations) conducting business in the jurisdiction must first obtain a business license, which

usually requires filling out the proper forms and payment of a periodic fee.

If you wish to conduct business under a fictitious business name or trade name, some jurisdictions require that you obtain permission from the licensing board to use a particular fictitious business name, while other jurisdictions allow you to use a fictitious name as long as it is not false, misleading or deceptive. In the case of the sole proprietor (an individual), a fictitious business name is generally considered to be a name that does not include the surname of the individual (e.g., Magnolia Street Counseling) or a name that suggests the existence of additional owners (Alice Z. Jones and Associates). Additionally, some jurisdictions require that persons using a fictitious business name file a statement with an agency of government, and publish in a newspaper of general circulation a notice which states the true name of the owner of the named business.

Some jurisdictions may also require that those doing business under a fictitious business name disclose to the client, prior to the commencement of treatment, the true name of the licensee (owner) and the fact that the licensee is a licensed marriage and family therapist. Such disclosure is appropriate and wise, even if not required by law or regulation. For example, when marriage and family therapists (MFTs) and others practice in what might be termed a "loose group" (advertising to the public as the XYZ Counseling Center while each of the therapists is actually conducting a sole proprietorship), it is important that the client understand who is ultimately responsible (legally and ethically) for the care being provided. In other words, who owns the business where treatment is being rendered? These kind of "loose group" arrangements can potentially be problematic since the therapists could be found to be operating under a de facto partnership arrangement. Therapists should exercise caution when entering into these types of arrangements; consultation with a local attorney is advisable.

Another form of doing business is the partnership, where two or more practitioners co-own the business and split profits and losses, usually pursuant to a written partnership agreement. The independence of the sole proprietorship is lost when doing business as a partnership, because each partner will have some right to determine how all aspects of the business are conducted. From a liability standpoint, since partners generally act as agents of the partnership, each partner is liable for the negligent acts of the other partners. It is usually unlawful for a marriage and family therapist to be in a partnership with a physician or a psychologist, since the only people who can lawfully receive money for medical services or psychological services are physicians or psychologists, respectively. Thus, most partnerships are between professionals holding the same license.

Many jurisdictions have passed laws that allow for the formation of professional corporations. The most important caveat with respect to the professional corporation (which can usually be formed by one or more licensees) is that, unlike a regular general business corporation, formed primarily to limit the liability of the individual owners (shareholders), the professional corporation usually does not limit the liability of the health care practitioner for the practitioner's own professional negligence.

Legislatures have deemed such a limitation of liability as being against public policy. Similarly, limited liability companies may not be a lawful option for health care practitioners in many jurisdictions.

Some jurisdictions allow for interdisciplinary professional corporations. For example, a physician is allowed to be a shareholder or employee of an MFT corporation and an MFT can be an owner (shareholder) or employee in a medical corporation under California law. The significance of this, from a business standpoint, is that an MFT Professional Corporation can lawfully deliver and bill for medical services rendered by a physician. (Remember, each jurisdiction has its own laws and regulations, so legal consultation is required.) Applicable law may require the name of the corporation to contain certain words or language and may require that the corporation register with the Board (State). It is important to determine whether applicable law allows for the professional corporation to do business under a fictitious name, and whether or not other requirements (e.g., filings, disclosures) exist.

Generally, unless a private practitioner has been advised that there are tax advantages (e.g., the ability to shelter more income) to incorporation, or unless there is a desire to co-own an interdisciplinary practice, incorporation may not be a compelling option. While professional incorporation may limit some kinds of liability (for example, if the client slips and falls on a defective rug in the therapist's office), it appears that such limited benefit is not by itself sufficient to convince most therapists to incorporate. Malpractice and related insurance coverage provides therapists with protection in case they are held liable for professional negligence or for negligently maintaining their premises.

FEE SETTING

One of the disclosures that must be made to a client, prior to the commencement of therapy, is the fee to be charged for the services that are to be rendered. Many therapists make this disclosure as part of a more general disclosure statement required by applicable law or dictated by sound and ethical professional practice. Therapists are generally free to set their own fees in accordance with what they think is appropriate for the clientele they expect to see and the services to be rendered. The importance of being clear when it comes to the issue of fees cannot be over emphasized. Some therapists choose to make clear to clients that if they are unable to continue to pay the agreed-upon fee, the therapist may terminate therapy (before a large arrearage accumulates) and refer the client to a low-cost counseling center or an appropriate governmental agency. It is, of course, possible that the therapist may choose to lower the fee (or charge nothing) and continue to see the client. If the client is suicidal or otherwise seriously impaired, ethics and prudence may dictate that treatment should continue, at least for some period of time. Otherwise, the therapist may be dealing with an allegation of abandonment.

If a therapist decides to raise fees at a given point in the development of the therapist's practice, there are two ways that is usually done. One is to raise the fee only for new clients. Some believe that raising fees during the course of therapy is exploitive because

the client is not in a good bargaining position when confronted with the request for additional money from the therapist. The AAMFT Code of Ethics provides that clients are to be given reasonable notice of any changes in fees or other charges. Fees should probably not be raised during the course of therapy unless the client has been informed, in advance of commencing treatment, of the possibility that fees and charges may increase. It is helpful if the therapist also lets the client know that fees will not increase more than once a year, and that the amount of the increase will not exceed a specified percentage.

Many therapists want to adopt a "sliding fee scale." Depending on the nature of the practice, a sliding fee scale is often impractical and awkward for private practitioners. It is more likely to be used in nonprofit and charitable corporations, where the fee to be charged can be determined by the income level of the client and the family. Private practitioners in most professions generally charge a set fee - their usual and customary fee. They are free to make exceptions and see someone for a lower fee or for no fee.

Setting a "usual and customary fee," with the right to make exceptions, is simple and easy to administer. It lets clients know what you think your time and ability are worth. When dealing with insurers and other payers, it provides consistency to your profile. If fees vary, based upon the economic circumstances of the client, including the presence or absence of insurance coverage, insurers may take the position that your fees are being artificially and improperly raised when there is insurance coverage. Depending upon the facts and circumstances, this kind of billing practice may constitute insurance fraud.

LIABILITY/INSURANCE

Therapists and other practitioners are liable for their negligent or intentional acts or omissions that cause harm to the client. Generally, in order to avoid liability, a therapist must act as a reasonably prudent practitioner holding the same license would have acted under like or similar circumstances. Generally, honest errors in judgment do not necessarily constitute negligence or result in liability. Employers are usually liable for the negligent acts of their employees. A supervisor can be held liable for the supervisor's own negligence in providing supervision and, depending on applicable law and the facts of the specific situation, can also be held vicariously liable for the negligence of the supervisee. Before deciding to take on supervisees, therapists should consider the advantages and disadvantages, and should take steps to manage the associated risks (e.g. maintain high professional standards, create and adhere to policies and procedures, create and adhere to supervision contracts). Similarly, therapists who employ others can be held liable, through the doctrine of respondeat superior, for the actions of their employees. The doctrine of respondeat superior generally means that employers can be held responsible for the acts of employees performing within the scope of their employment.

Active private practitioners must **at all times** have insurance coverage for malpractice (professional liability) claims or lawsuits. Therapists should not skimp when it comes to protecting themselves with the maximum coverage they can obtain. It gives therapists peace of mind and prepares them for the worst-case scenario. Most malpractice insurers also provide coverage for legal representation at depositions and at disciplinary proceedings before a regulatory board.

Do not allow your policy to lapse for any period of time. A therapist risks a suit for negligence that occurred during any interruption in coverage. They became personally exposed to not only a monetary judgment against them, but also to the rather substantial costs of an adequate legal defense. This can also happen to practitioners who put their licenses on inactive status and cancel their insurance. Shortly after doing so, a former client contacts the therapist during a crisis and the therapist steps in to help, ever so briefly. In such a situation, the therapist is "bare" (personally exposed) for the negligence that may occur during the period the therapist is without professional liability coverage.

ADVERTISING

Most businesses, including small health care practices, implement an advertising plan or strategy of some kind. Most jurisdictions allow health care practitioners to advertise in any way or with any medium, but prohibit advertising that is false, fraudulent, misleading, or deceptive. Therapists should also be aware of any advertising guidelines or requirements found in applicable codes of ethics.

Some jurisdictions have imposed a variety of other requirements, such as a mandate to use the license number in any advertisement. Also, those who conduct business under a fictitious business name may be required to make disclosures regarding the actual ownership of the business. With respect to advertising about fees or the costs for services, some laws prohibit the use of certain language (e.g., "lowest fees").

Chapter 2: Forms for Use in Your Practice

There are many sources for practice forms. Some jurisdictions require that a client record contain specific forms or specific content. Some jurisdictions require disclosure forms that provide specific information to clients. An informed consent form can be the basis for your agreement with a client and limit your risk for records requests and court appearances.

You can use an office policies document to state your records retention and destruction policy. You can supplement your informed consent document with additional information when the client is a minor child and the parents are divorced. Some jurisdictions grant specific rights to non-custodial parents with respect to the records of a minor child. Some jurisdictions specify the amounts that can be charged for record production at the request of a client. Some jurisdictions permit minors to seek therapy without parental consent.

INFORMED CONSENT

An informed consent/consent to treat/ disclosure document is strategic documenta- tion: a document that demonstrates that what the practitioner did was appropriate, correct and required.

Informed consent is a concept that is generally used to advise clients of the limitations on confidentiality and fee structure. A typical informed consent document might state the instances where the therapist would have to disclose otherwise confidential information (e.g. child sexual abuse, elder abuse, a threat of violence of a third party, or suicide.) The

typical consent form might then discuss the policy regarding payment and whether fees would be charged for canceled sessions and so forth.

As an advice document, the informed consent would be the appropriate time and place to advise couples, families or groups that all therapy participants have to agree to a waiver of confidentiality. It would also be appropriate at that time to discuss the therapist's partici- pation in any litigation that might result in the future and secure the client's agreement.

Whether a client's agreement not to involve the therapist in future litigation is enforceable is a different issue. The judicial process is separate from and often not controlled by the client. For example, a client may file a lawsuit, and mental or emotional distress may be an element of damages claimed. The defendant in the lawsuit will make demands on the therapist for records and testimony to show that the client's distress is unrelated to the defendant's actions. The client has not involved the therapist and has not breached the agreement.

A therapist can certainly use a non-litigation section in the informed consent document to identify fees and charges for the therapist's time and expenses if a subpoena is issued.

Even though a court may not interpret your informed consent document as a legally binding contract, some courts may give consideration to the document when making a determination about whether to quash a subpoena.

At a minimum your informed consent document should address the following areas:

- Nature, purpose, and anticipated course of services

- Limits of confidentiality

- Explanation of client identity/no secrets policy

- Records requests/client's right of access to records/privacy policy

- Fees and billing arrangements (including collection practices and charges for court)

- Insurance reimbursement, if applicable

- Emergency procedures for contacting therapist

- Policies on use of technology (e.g. email, social media)

Remember that applicable laws and regulations may have other or additional requirements for a disclosure or informed consent document.

Chapter 3: Keeping Clinical Records - Legal and Ethical Issues

WHY KEEP RECORDS?

Aside from the fact that it is likely required, it is good business practice to keep records of the transactions and occurrences within any business. With respect to behavioral health care professions, the need for good record keeping is more important, since the behavioral health of a client is involved, as well as significant marital, family, and other interpersonal relationships. Some therapists say that they keep minimal records in order to protect the privacy of the client. There may be more protection for the therapist and the client from laws governing confidentiality and client privilege, and, for those therapists practicing in the United States, the Health Insurance Portability and Accountability Act of 1996 (HIPAA).

Good record keeping is important both to clients and to therapists. Clients may need to prove their mental status or that they suffered emotional distress or other impairment. The need to do so may arise in a custody or visitation proceeding, in a civil lawsuit for damages, in a workers' compensation or disability case, for a security clearance, or for some other reason. Clients depend upon their therapists to keep adequate and accurate records, which can provide proof that the client is, for example, being treated for a particular mental disorder. Additionally, clients have a right to expect that, if they were to obtain treatment at a later time from another practitioner, the records from the prior therapist would be available to the new therapist, if needed.

Good record keeping can help the therapist establish that the therapist acted appropriately if sued by the client for negligence, or in a disciplinary proceeding by a regulatory board or an investigation by an ethics committee. When a client attempts or commits suicide, for example, or causes physical harm to others, the therapist is sometimes the target of an investigation or lawsuit to determine whether or not the therapist acted appropriately. A member of a couple or family receiving services may try to hold the therapist responsible for a divorce or separation or for the loss of custody or visitation rights. Well-documented records can help the therapist prove that the therapist acted reasonably.

CONTENT OF RECORDS

Some jurisdictions specify the content required to be in records maintained by MFTs and/ or other licensed health professionals, while other jurisdictions take a different approach and leave actual content to the discretion of the therapist. HIPAA's Privacy Rule, in creating a right of access to information in the record, lists documents that, if they exist, are available to the client: medication prescription and monitoring, counseling session start and stop times, the modalities and frequencies of treatment furnished, results of clinical tests, and any summary of the following items: diagnosis, functional status, the treatment plan, symptoms, prognosis, and progress to date.

Helpful documentation includes any consultation had with other practitioners who have confirmed or expressed support for the herapist's treatment approach. Both the fact of the consultation, and the substance of it, can often help to prove that the therapist was not negligent. Even though professional opinion and judgment may differ, the therapist may have acted competently and appropriately, albeit not perfectly. Another useful thing to document is the fact that the therapist has referred the client to a physician for a medical exam, or to a psychiatrist for medication, or to other licensed practitioners for testing or other services. It is also important to accurately document all billings and payments so as to avoid fee disputes with clients.

Therapists must often balance competing interests when determining record content. Sometimes a therapist may want to omit or excise a name from the record in order to protect the client or a third party. If a client were having an extramarital affair, for example, the client and the therapist might be more comfortable if the name of the paramour was omitted from the record.

Because record keeping requirements can vary across jurisdictions, therapists are advised to refer to their applicable laws.

WHO OWNS THE RECORDS?

Some jurisdictions are very specific that the mental health professional owns the record, while a client has a right to access the record or get a copy of the record.

Under HIPAA's Privacy Rule, clients have certain rights with respect to the mental health record. Most jurisdictions also give clients rights to records. Under HIPAA's Privacy Rule, a client is entitled to inspect and copy the protected health information in the client's

mental health record. Don't forget that if the client has more than one participant, under AAMFT's Code of Ethics, the participants who are not requesting the records must sign an authorization to disclose the information.

Questions related to client access to records are best addressed as part of the informed consent discussion at the beginning of the therapeutic relationship. A Notice of Privacy Practices, required for HIPAA covered entities, might avoid surprising the client when, for example, you require a request for records to be made in writing or paid for in advance. Even if you are not a "covered provider," and required by HIPAA to provide a Notice of Privacy Practices, you might want to consider making the specifics of a request for records part of your informed consent document.

Ownership of the record sometimes becomes an issue when clients request the destruction of treatment records. A client who requests that the therapist destroy all treatment records on termination of the relationship is probably concerned about privacy and confidentiality, or upset about the results or direction of the therapy. While the client can request and receive a copy of most of the contents of the file, the client cannot direct destruction of the record.

Record ownership can also be an issue when an employee of an agency or private practice leaves the employment voluntarily or is fired. A rule of thumb is that clients can be seen as clients of the agency, rather than clients of any particular therapist employed by the agency. As such, employees may not be entitled to "take" clients or their records. If the employee negotiates with the employer so that clients are permitted to leave the agency and follow the therapist, the agency or other entity should keep a copy of the record in case some question arises about the client's treatment while a client of the agency. If the client remains with the agency, the departing therapist has no need for a copy of the record. Indeed, it is grounds for quashing a subpoena for records that the therapist does not have the records requested, and that the subpoena should be directed to the agency or entity.

If the relationship between the therapist and agency or entity is that of principal and independent contractor, it is more likely than not that the independent contractor agreement addresses the issue of record ownership and whether therapists will be permitted to "take" clients with them should the contractual relationship come to an end or be terminated.

HIPAA PSYCHOTHERAPY NOTES

For those therapists practicing in the United States, "psychotherapy notes," as defined by HIPAA, are a frequent topic of discussion. Generally speaking, when a client makes a request to access the treatment record, under HIPAA the therapist is permitted to exclude access to psychotherapy notes.

The section of HIPAA's Privacy Rule that excludes psychotherapy notes can be found at 45 Code of Federal Regulations Section 164.524. It says that an individual is entitled to a copy of protected health information (essentially anything with a name or identifying number on it) except Psychotherapy Notes.

Psychotherapy notes are very specifically defined, but can be shorthanded to any recording by you, the therapist, of the content of a therapy session. Psychotherapy notes exclude medication prescription and monitoring, counseling session start and stop times, modalities and frequencies of treatment, the results of clinical tests, and any summary of diagnosis, functional status, treatment plan, symptoms, prognosis, and progress (see 45 CFR 164.501).

Psychotherapy notes must be separated from the rest of the record to be classified and protected as psychotherapy notes. It is also important for therapists to understand that in the context of litigation, psychotherapy notes may be discoverable (e.g. subject to subpoena, produced by order of the court).

SAFE MAINTENANCE OF RECORDS/DESTRUCTION

Therapists have a duty to protect the privacy of client records. Thus, therapists must take care to safeguard records, and to the extent possible, prevent records from being lost, stolen, or viewed by "third parties." For paper records, this usually translates into keeping records in a locked file cabinet in the therapist's office. The therapist's office also should be locked when it is not being used. Client files should not be left in public areas, where they may be seen or taken. Whether records are kept on a computer or otherwise, the records should only be available to those who need to have access in order to carry out the therapist's business. Computer screens should be placed and used in a manner that does not allow viewing by others. Computer records should be regularly and promptly backed up so that they are not lost due to technical error or failure.

A common mistake is permitting records to be taken from the premises where they belong (e.g. a private practice, clinic, or nonprofit organization). This is often done in order to accommodate an intern or trainee who is receiving off-site supervision. If the supervision cannot take place onsite, it is important to take certain precautions. For instance, if records are to be taken for the benefit of the supervision, take a copy rather than the original file. Ideally, take only portions of a file, or alter information regarding the client's identity. Therapists who transport records should keep the records under their personal control at all times, and not leave the records in a car or in someone's office or residence.

When records are destroyed, after passage of the appropriate amount of time, they should be destroyed in a manner that preserves confidentiality (e.g. shredding, burning). Records should not be placed in a trash bag for disposal by others, nor should records be abandoned or left behind.

WHAT IF THE RECORDS ARE LOST, STOLEN OR DESTROYED?

If records are lost or stolen, the therapist may want to reconstruct the records for treatment purposes. Of course, the ability to reconstruct will depend upon the complexity of the case and the length of time that the client has been in treatment. Records from former providers can usually be obtained again. The primary fear of the therapist when records are lost or stolen is that confidential information will be seen by someone, thus violating the client's right to privacy and confidentiality. Therapists may face the dilemma of whether or not to tell the client of the loss as soon as discovered, or whether to make some attempt to recover the records before telling the client.

Therapists are often reluctant to tell the client, either because they don't want the client to be alarmed and suffer emotional distress, or because they do not want the client to blame them for improperly handling or protecting the records. There may be times when the client is in such mental or emotional condition as to warrant the therapist keeping the loss of records from the client, at least for some period of time. It is important to make sure that this reason is only used when supported by the clinical evidence, and not as part of an effort to hide the fact that privacy may have been compromised.

The facts of each situation should be evaluated, but consider choosing prompt notification of the client. This may, in some cases, subject the therapist to some liability for the negligent handling or maintenance of the records, but in many cases, the therapist may have done nothing wrong. Perhaps there was a burglary hurricane or other natural disaster. Prompt disclosure to the client reduces the likelihood that the client would question why the therapist kept the loss secret.

Therapists are advised to also look to applicable laws for guidance in situations where client information may have been lost, stolen, or otherwise potentially subjected to unauthorized access. For example, therapists bound by HIPAA should be knowledgeable about the HIPAA Breach Notification Rule.

Prompt and full disclosure is easy when the therapist has not acted negligently. Suppose, however, that a licensed supervisor or employer allows a trainee or intern to take records from the premises and bring them to an off-site supervisor. What if the intern negligently protected the records and now they are missing? Perhaps the intern left the records in an unlocked car or in a briefcase that was misplaced. And further, perhaps a copy of the records was not made. Is the supervisor or employer going to want to immediately notify the client of the missing records and the details of their loss? The supervisor or employer faced with such a dilemma will want to consult with legal counsel, who will help to evaluate the situation and to hopefully minimize the harm done to the client and to the employer or supervisor.

WHAT IF THE THERAPIST MOVES OR RETIRES?

Some jurisdictions require a therapist to publicize, usually in the local newspaper, a relocation from the area or retirement so that former clients who may need their records will know, or be more likely to know, the location of the records. With respect to clients who are in treatment at the time the therapist decides to move or retire, therapists should notify clients as early as possible and should document such action in their records.

In jurisdictions that have no requirements for notice of a move or of retirement, therapists should consider either publication of a notice in a newspaper, or direct notice by letter to the former clients. If using direct notice by letter, consider whether contacting the former client risks compromising the client's privacy or confidentiality.

In most jurisdictions, licensees are required to notify their licensing board of any change of business address. Additionally, retired licensees can put their licenses on inactive status. Thus, a licensing board can usually help a client find a therapist who has moved or retired.

If you are required to notify your licensing board of a change of business address, and if there is no requirement to publish the fact of the move or retirement, notice to former clients may be unnecessary. Of course, if you have retained the records as long as required, they can be destroyed. In that case, the issue of notice to the client is moot. There is generally no requirement that the client be notified prior to a lawful destruction of records.

Chapter 4: Unpaid Balance Issues

Occasionally therapists may have to deal with issues that arise when a client has been permitted to accumulate an unpaid balance. This chapter will focus on two specific issues: withholding records from a client with an unpaid balance and seeking to collect an unpaid balance.

Taking into account specific requirements in their jurisdictions and applicable codes of ethics, therapists should include language in their informed consent documentation and office policies that discusses financial arrangements with clients, including issues related to nonpayment of fees.

When a client who owes fees makes a request for clinical records, a therapist may see this as an opportunity to obtain some leverage in the struggle to obtain payment and could be tempted to make fulfillment of the client's request contingent upon payment. However, therapists are typically advised to provide the records in accordance with applicable laws and ethical requirements, while continuing to use other legitimate means to resolve the debt.

From a business standpoint, a therapist has the right to pursue payment for services rendered and to use legitimate means for seeking collection when payment is past due. Generally speaking, when a therapist is seeking to collect an unpaid balance, providing reasonable notice to clients of the intent to seek collection is advisable and may also be required by applicable laws or codes of ethics.

One approach may be to send the client a letter with return receipt requested (to show the client received it), making a demand for payment of the outstanding balance, and stating that if the therapist does not hear from the client by a specific date (three to four weeks is usually enough notice), the therapist will turn the account over for collection or file a suit in small claims court.

Therapists may also need to attend to any confidentiality issues presented by seeking to collect an unpaid balance. Generally speaking, therapists should disclose the minimum amount of information necessary and likely do not need to include clinical information when seeking to collect an unpaid balance.

Laws governing the collection of unpaid balances may vary across jurisdictions, so therapists are advised to seek consultation with a local attorney prior to undertaking any steps to collect an unpaid balance.

Chapter 5: Regulatory Board Complaints

For those MFTs practicing in jurisdictions that regulate the practice of marriage and family therapy, the possibility of facing a complaint to a regulatory board exists. One function of a regulatory board is the investigation of complaints against license holders. A regulatory board can receive complaints from many sources including liability insurance companies, professional associations, law enforcement agencies, or regulatory boards in other jurisdictions. Any client, family member or concerned citizen can file a complaint with a regulatory board alleging that a license holder has violated the licensing law or board regulations.

Each board has its own rules and regulations for investigating complaints against license holders. Some investigations involve sending a copy of the complaint and asking the licensee to respond. This means the licensee may have to sift through the complaint and try and determine what board rule or regulation may have been violated. Other investigations involve board or staff review of the complaint and a letter outlining the facts of the complaint and how those facts state a violation of the licensing law or regulations.

Although easier said than done, if you receive a complaint from your board, don't panic. The first step is to make sure that you are actually the therapist involved. The complainant or the board could have made a mistake. If you recognize that the complaint is from someone you know or treated, locate the file and refresh your recollection about the case. You may have documents that refute the complaint. For example, a former client claims you breached his confidentiality and you have a signed release in the file.

Contacting your professional liability insurer is advisable if you've received notice of a complaint. Depending on your policy and coverage, your insurer may make a referral to a local attorney to assist you in responding to the complaint. Consultation with a local attorney prior to responding to a complaint can be very helpful to understand your jurisdiction's complaint process and to get specific advice to aid you in your response.

Chapter 6: Duty to Report Colleague

At some point in a therapist's career, the therapist may be confronted with a situation involving known or alleged concerns about another therapist's conduct. A therapist may become aware of a colleague's potentially problematic conduct in various ways. Based on calls to AAMFT, the following ways appear to be most prevalent:

- The therapist learns of the colleague's conduct through reports from other colleagues, direct observation of the colleague's conduct, or through the colleague's report directly to the therapist;

- The therapist learns of the colleague's conduct through reports from clients; or

- The therapist learns of the colleague's conduct because the colleague is a client of the therapist and the colleague discloses the conduct to the therapist.

Regardless of how therapists learn of a colleague's potentially problematic conduct, therapists may wonder whether they have a duty to report a colleague to regulatory boards, professional associations, etc. At the time of publication, AAMFT's Code of Ethics requires MFTs to comply with applicable laws. In this type of situation, local law (e.g. state, provincial) will likely set forth applicable requirements. Some jurisdictions do have laws that discuss reporting colleagues or other licensees, while other jurisdictions may not. It is important for MFTs to be clear that, at the time of publication, AAMFT's Code of Ethics does not impose an independent reporting requirement in an instance where a colleague has engaged in unprofessional or unethical conduct.

When therapists learn of the problematic conduct through clients or a colleague-client, therapists will need to consider client confidentiality issues. Therapists are advised to review applicable laws carefully to determine whether any applicable reporting obligations would override the client's or colleague-client's confidentiality rights.

When the colleague is a client and there is no mandate to report, therapists might consider approaching the situation clinically and working towards a self-report. Certainly therapists want to avoid breaking confidentiality, even if therapy has terminated, given the absence of a clear legal mandate to do so.

If a therapist learns of a colleague's potentially problematic conduct outside of the therapeutic relationship and if a report is not required, another option to consider is approaching the colleague in the spirit of "friendly remonstrance" in keeping with the tradition of self-regulation and maintaining high standards within the profession. Immunity is often conferred by statutes that require or encourage colleagues to report the unethical behavior or impaired practice of others. In order for that immunity to be effective, however, you may need first-hand knowledge of the behavior and will need to comply with your jurisdiction's reporting requirements (e.g. pay close attention to where a report is to be directed).

You are encouraged to report unethical behavior of colleagues. However, because you are not mandated to do so under the current AAMFT Code of Ethics, it would not be a violation of the Code if you did not report your colleague to AAMFT or another appropriate venue, so long as you are in compliance with applicable laws.

Chapter 7: Incorporating Technology into Your Practice

In today's world, therapists have the opportunity to incorporate various technologies into their practices to improve efficiency of their practices and support competent, quality, effective client care.

Common areas of practice where technology may be used include payment, delivery, and documentation of services. Across all areas of practice, therapists need to attend to confidentiality and security of clients' protected health information, as well as any additional legal and ethical mandates.

The technology available today has outpaced some of the laws that regulate the profession of marriage and family therapy, and behavioral healthcare in general. For example, it is not uncommon for therapists to inquire about whether they can offer services to clients located in other jurisdictions. Prior to offering such services, therapists must be knowledgeable about, and comply with, any applicable licensing laws. If a therapist provides services to a client located in a jurisdiction where the therapist is not licensed, the therapist may run the risk of being found to have engaged in unlicensed practice. Whether such a finding is made will depend on the specific facts of the situation and the applicable licensing laws in question.

Technology has the potential to increase efficiency of practices and access to care, but also has the potential to lead therapists into trouble. When incorporating technology into their practices, therapists should be knowledgeable about any and all legal and ethical mandates.

Selecting appropriate vendors, understanding the risks to clients' protected health information, implementing appropriate policies and procedures to safeguard that information, and being knowledgeable about legal and ethical mandates in this area will go a long way in ensuring the successful incorporation of technology into your practice.

PART II:
THE THERAPIST
AND THE CLIENT

Chapter 1: Selected Issues in Confidentiality

The cornerstone principle of the various mental health professions is confidentiality. This legal and ethical principle is critical to successful work with clients, since clients must be assured of confidentiality in order for them to share with their therapists the most private, intimate and sometimes embarrassing details of their lives. The likelihood of clinical success is increased when the client feels comfortable sharing such details with the therapist. Clients put a lot of trust in their therapists, especially with respect to confidentiality. A wrongful breach of confidentiality not only subjects the therapist to civil and administrative liability, but also can have a lasting effect on the client's mental health and how the client views the profession.

SOME GENERAL RULES

The first general rule to remember is that you should not release information about a client without the client's signed authorization. Another general rule is that when you release confidential information, only release the minimum amount of information necessary to accomplish the purpose of the release. A third general rule to remember is that when in doubt, resist releasing information and opt in favor of maintaining confidentiality. Ordinarily, there is greater risk in releasing information without the client's authorization then there is in preserving confidentiality. Since these are "general" rules, there are exceptions.

With respect to requiring a client's signed authorization prior to the release of confidential information, there are times when therapists must disclose information without a signed authorization and times when they may do this. Child abuse and elder abuse reporting laws are well-recognized mandatory exceptions to the general rule. Permissive disclosures would typically include cases where a therapist, among other things, has reasonable cause to believe that the client is a danger to self or to others. Additionally, certain forms of child abuse and elder abuse may not require reports but may permit reports to be made. Under some laws (e.g. HIPAA), therapists may be permitted to make disclosures without the client's written authorization for purposes of the provider's treatment, payment and health care operations.

Releasing the minimum amount of information necessary to accomplish the purpose of the release is a common practice that has been adopted in HIPAA regulations. The therapist confronts this when insurance companies want to see a client's entire file. Therapists should attempt to narrow the insurer's request and to provide only the relevant portion of the records. In situations where a warning has to be (or may be) made to the intended victim of the client's threatened violence, as in the Tarasoff case, the warning should generally be concise, direct and limited in scope. However, the minimum necessary rule is inapplicable in certain circumstances. For instance, it doesn't apply to releases of confidential information by a health care provider for purposes of treatment of the client, where full and complete information is helpful to proper treatment. It doesn't apply to a client's request for a copy of his/her records, and it generally doesn't apply in cases where there is a written authorization.

With respect to the general principle of "when in doubt, resist disclosure," therapists will typically not get in trouble if they resist when in doubt, as long as they make reasonable attempts to ascertain the appropriateness or necessity of disclosure. This principle comes into play with great frequency (and with frequent mistakes by therapists) when an attorney asks the therapist to make and sign a declaration, usually in a divorce/custody proceeding, about one of the parties, or when a client asks the therapist to write a letter to the attorney. While the facts and circumstances vary in these kind of proceedings, the therapist should make sure that the file contains written permission from all of those who might argue that they were entitled to confidentiality. (For a discussion on privilege, a topic closely related to confidentiality, refer to Chapter 2 in Section III of this book.)

THE FACT OF THE RELATIONSHIP

You should treat the fact of the relationship as confidential. In other words, you should not tell anyone who your clients are or acknowledge that you are treating a particular client. It is not unusual for a therapist to be asked by a law enforcement officer, some other governmental official, or perhaps by a family member, whether or not the therapist is treating a particular client. The answer, given in your own words and style, is "none of your business." If one were not treating the person inquired about, the therapist does not necessarily have to acknowledge that fact, and might decline to respond to the inquiry. Simply put, the identity of the client is confidential.

Some may take issue with this principle, since it is not unusual for therapists and counseling agencies to have waiting rooms where clients see other clients and where names are sometimes called out. Clients may also be seen entering the offices of therapists, and in smaller communities, the identity of such clients may be apparent. To arrange office visits otherwise, would probably make people think that there is something wrong with going to a therapist's office and would increase the stigma of mental health treatment even more.

Another thing to consider about the fact of the relationship (as opposed to the content of the therapy) is whether or not you have the client's permission to write to them, call them, or otherwise communicate with them at their home or at some other place. Perhaps the spouse or partner does not know that the client is in therapy, and perhaps the client is not ready to reveal this fact. A letter or bill sent by the therapist may be seen by the spouse or partner and may cause problems for the client, even if it is marked "confidential." Yet another consideration is whether or not the client would want you to acknowledge them should you unexpectedly bump into them in a public place. These issues should be considered, discussed, and clarified with clients early in the relationship.

The fact of the relationship comes into play with respect to pursuing a client or ex-client for monies owed. Some laws contain provisions that clarify that it is not a violation of confidentiality or of the psychotherapist-patient privilege to sue a client (usually in small claims court) for monies owed. Similarly, therapists and other health practitioners sometimes send unpaid bills to a collection agency. (Use of a collection agency should, if possible, be avoided and only be done with care and with prior notice to the client.) Generally, these actions do not constitute a breach of confidentiality so long as the disclosures made reveal only the fact of the relationship and the amount owed, and not the content or substance of the therapy. If the law were otherwise (each jurisdiction's law varies to some degree, so therapists must determine what their jurisdiction allows), therapists would be unable to collect monies that were lawfully due them.

CRIMES OF THE CLIENT

Each jurisdiction's laws usually address the issue of confidentiality and specify the exceptions to confidentiality. It is important to be familiar with the laws in the jurisdiction where you practice so that violations of confidentiality do not occur. Generally (but not always) the past crimes of a client, revealed to the therapist during therapy, are confidential. Many clients tell therapists about past crimes, such as possession or sale of controlled substances, driving while intoxicated, stealing from an employer, or committing a violent crime. Therapists routinely keep such information confidential. Of course, child abuse and neglect reporting laws and elder or dependent adult abuse reporting laws are well known exceptions to the general rule.

Prospective violence, either communicated to the therapist or assessed by the therapist, presents a different situation. Under these circumstances, disclosure by the therapist may be mandated or permitted, depending upon applicable law. In short, therapists are usually at least permitted to break confidentiality when the client is in such mental or emotional condition as to be a danger to self or to others, and disclosure is necessary to prevent the threatened danger. Imminent threats of violence against readily identifiable victims, communicated directly to the therapist by the client, may trigger (in some jurisdictions) the so-called "duty to warn" or "duty to protect".

AIDS/HIV

Suppose a client tells the therapist that the client is HIV-positive or has been diagnosed with AIDS and that the client is engaging in unprotected sex with the client's partner.

Is the risk of the partner's infection a circumstance in which confidentiality can be broken? Some states have broadened the Tarasoff standard by enacting legislation that allows physicians, under certain conditions, to disclose the status of a patient to sexual (or needle sharing) partners of that patient. For mental health professionals, however, there may not be any specific legal directives regarding confidentiality and the protection of third parties from AIDS or HIV infection.

Some have argued that there is or ought to be a "duty to warn," like in the famed Tarasoff decision, but others have pointed out that "Tarasoff situations" involve serious (and imminent) threats of violence, communicated by clients to therapists, against readily identifiable others.

Some have also argued that while no duty to warn may exist, therapists are permitted to warn because the client is, under circumstances where no disclosure of the condition is made by the client to a partner, a "danger to others." However, the Tarasoff "danger to others" standards must usually be as the result of the mental or emotional condition of the client. The danger here is usually the result of a physical disease or condition that may or may not be transmitted, not as the result of a mental or emotional condition. Additionally, the Tarasoff "danger to others" is usually the danger of physical violence, such as homicide. Even if the client was in such a mental or emotional condition as to be dangerous—if the client were to tell the therapist that the client's goal is to infect as many people as possible—it is arguable that confidentiality should be maintained (unless there is specific statutory instruction to the contrary).

Therapists who find themselves in this type of situation should look to the laws of their jurisdiction to determine whether any reporting obligations exist. Therapists can also act by, among other things, discussing the importance of full disclosure by the client to partners and by discussing other possible changes of client behavior. The Centers for Disease Control and Prevention in the United States has program information directed to partner counseling and referral for HIV/AIDS prevention. One recommended method is to have the therapist be present when the client notifies the partner. Another method recommends that the therapist and client agree on a date and, if the client has not notified the partner by that date, the client agrees that the therapist should notify the partner. The agreement may serve as a waiver of the client's confidentiality rights if the client fails to notify the partner.

OTHER CLIENT DISCLOSURES

Other types of client disclosures that could potentially trigger an exception to confidentiality include disclosures related to the viewing or possessing of child pornography and disclosures about threats to property of another. It is imperative that therapists know their jurisdiction's laws surrounding confidentiality and exceptions to confidentiality.

Chapter 2: Duty to Warn and/or Protect

You will probably face a situation sometime during your professional careers when you will be treating a client who presents a physical danger to others, to self, or to the property of others. In such situations, the dilemma is whether or not the therapist is required or permitted to break confidentiality in order to protect the client or others from harm.

The duty of confidentiality for mental health practitioners is both an ethical and legal imperative. Applicable laws require confidentiality and provide for disciplinary action, including revocation of license, for violations of the duty. Breaching confidentiality also subjects a practitioner to liability for damages in malpractice suits. The codes of ethics for all mental health professions address the issue of confidentiality, and membership in a professional association can be terminated or otherwise limited for violations of the duty. The duty of confidentiality is not absolute. Therapists are well aware, for example, of their duties to report suspected child abuse and elder or dependent adult abuse.

The famous *Tarasoff v. Regents of the University of California* decision created a new duty for California therapists in 1976. Many other jurisdictions follow this California decision, and some states have enacted laws that codify the so-called "Tarasoff duty." Laws vary across jurisdictions, so therapists should know what the "duty" is in the jurisdictions in which they practice.

The key language from Tarasoff states that "[w]hen a therapist determines, or pursuant to the standards of his profession should determine, that his client presents a serious danger of violence to another, he incurs an obligation to use reasonable care to protect the intended victim against such danger." "Serious danger of violence" is used rather than "danger of serious violence." In other words, the threat must be imminent – it is a serious threat rather than a mere "huffing and puffing" in a moment of anger or a conditional threat that may or may not be executed in the future.

It is not uncommon for therapists to ask what their duty is when a client tells them that someone else has communicated to the client a threat of violence against the client or a third party. The Tarasoff decision and most jurisdiction's laws are concerned with threatened violence by the client, not by some other party. Unless applicable law provides otherwise, this situation would require the therapist to keep the communication confidential.

Other variations on the classic "Tarasoff" situation include client threats against property and situations where a family member or friend might contact the therapist to report that the client has made some type of threat. Therapists must know the law in their jurisdiction on these issues so that they are prepared for these types of situations.

One other portion of the Tarasoff decision is instructive, since it reinforces the importance of confidentiality. The court stated: "We realize that the open and confidential character of psychotherapeutic dialogue encourages the client to express threats of violence, few of which are ever executed.

Certainly, a therapist should not be encouraged to routinely reveal such threats; such disclosures could seriously disrupt the client's relationship with his therapist and with the persons threatened. To the contrary, the therapist's obligations to his client require that he not disclose a confidence unless such disclosure is necessary to avert danger to others, and even then that he do so discreetly, and in a fashion that would preserve the privacy of his client to the fullest extent compatible with the prevention of the threatened danger."

Chapter 3: Mandatory Child Abuse and Neglect Reporting

A well-recognized exception to client confidentiality is the mandatory reporting of child abuse and neglect. Some jurisdictions have imposed similar reporting requirements in the case of elder abuse or neglect, or even dependent or vulnerable adult abuse or neglect. This chapter will focus on the mandatory reporting of child abuse or neglect.

Under the laws of most jurisdictions, MFTs, as mental health care professionals, are mandated reporters. It is critical that an MFT have detailed knowledge about the child abuse and neglect reporting laws, since a failure to report or failure to report within a specified time is often treated as a crime, and can lead to disciplinary action by the therapist's regulatory board and liability (money damages) in a civil lawsuit.

Most reporting laws provide immunity from civil and criminal liability for making a report. The immunity laws may even protect the therapist if the therapist was negligent in concluding that a report was required. Some states require that, in order to be entitled to the immunity, the mandated reporter must have acted "in good faith." While these immunity provisions do not necessarily prevent a therapist from being sued, they do provide the therapist the opportunity to assert immunity as a defense.

In most child abuse and neglect reporting laws, a child is defined as a person under the age of 18. One of the important issues involving age is the question of whether there is a requirement to report abuse of a person who is now an adult, but who tells the therapist about abuse occurring in the past when the client was under 18. The abuse could have taken place a few weeks ago or many years earlier. In some jurisdictions it is reasonably well established that there is no duty to report under such circumstances. In fact, if a report were made, the therapist might not be entitled to immunity, since it was not a report that was either required or authorized by the reporting law.

The standard for reporting child abuse or neglect differs somewhat across jurisdictions. Some jurisdictions use "reasonable cause to believe" as the standard while others use "reasonable suspicion" as the standard. Other statutes require the reporter to "know or suspect." It is helpful, especially when dealing with questionable reporting situations, to know the statutory standard. The basic question is whether you need a mere suspicion, a reasonable suspicion, or something closer to probable cause in order to be mandated to report child abuse.

"Physical abuse" of a child is usually considered to be a physical injury inflicted by other than accidental means. Depending upon applicable law, slapping, spanking or other non-severe forms of corporal punishment that result in no physical injury may not amount to child abuse. Reportable "sexual abuse" of a child usually includes sexual assault (e.g., rape, incest, sodomy, or oral copulation) and sexual exploitation (e.g., employment of a minor to perform obscene acts or assisting a child to engage in prostitution).

"Neglect" is generally defined as the neglectful treatment or maltreatment of a child by any person responsible for the child's welfare. It typically includes both acts and omissions. General neglect involves the negligent failure of the responsible person to provide adequate food, shelter, clothing, medical care, or supervision. Severe neglect involves the custodian's *intentional* failure to provide adequate food, clothing, shelter, medical care or supervision. In most states, neglect must be reported, whether general or severe.

With respect to "emotional abuse" or "mental suffering," there is usually no question about reporting severe emotional abuse—it generally will be mandated. Handcuffing a child to the bed or locking the child in a closet (where no physical injury is involved) is an example. Excessive scolding, punishment, blaming and belittlement for insufficient reasons may also be considered to be severe emotional abuse.

The time and manner of reporting varies from jurisdiction to jurisdiction. Generally, a report must be made immediately or as soon as possible by telephone or, in some jurisdictions, electronically. A written report may also be required to be made within a short period of time. Reports are usually required to be made to a designated child protective services agency or a law enforcement office such as the police or sheriff. The reporting duty is generally considered to be an individual duty and cannot be delegated. Some states have enacted laws that prevent employers of mandated reporters from taking sanctions against such employees who may make a report even though the employer has instructed that no report be made.

MANDATORY REPORTING AND INFORMED CONSENT

The duty to report should be one of the instances included in your "informed consent" document that may require a breach in confidentiality. Clients should be given notice that, as a mandatory reporter, you are required to breach confidentiality if clients disclose conduct that you are required by law to report.

MANDATORY REPORTING WHEN YOU'RE "OFF THE CLOCK"

Therapists may occasionally wonder about their reporting obligations when they observe or learn about suspected child abuse or neglect in their personal lives or when they are "off the clock," so to speak. In most cases, mandatory reporting laws require that the reporter have acquired the information in the course of practice of the profession. Consequently, when a therapist observes or learns of suspected child abuse or neglect in a non-professional capacity, a duty to report may not be triggered.

Because mandatory reporting obligations are largely matters of local law (e.g. state law, provincial law), it is critical that therapists know the law in their jurisdictions.

Chapter 4: Treating Children – Selected Legal and Ethical Issues

This section explores some of the common legal and ethical issues that may arise when a therapist agrees to treat a child. It provides some general guidance for navigating through this area of practice. Each jurisdiction may have its own law applicable to MFTs requiring something other than what is suggested or mentioned in this chapter. Therapists should always comply with the laws in their jurisdictions.

PARENTAL CONSENT TO TREATMENT

The general rule is that either parent has the right to obtain medical or mental health care for their minor children. Likewise, each parent has a general duty to care for the child, and, where necessary, to obtain needed medical or mental health care for the child. Therapists usually want to obtain the consent of both parents before agreeing to treat a child to avoid problems and disputes and to involve both parents in the treatment, where such involvement is appropriate.

There are, however, many circumstances (e.g., one parent incarcerated or otherwise out of the picture) where a therapist may appropriately and lawfully treat children with the consent of only one parent. Therapists who agree to treat under such circumstances must use good judgment in deciding whether the circumstances justify seeing the child with the consent of only one parent. The therapist must think of both the legal requirements of consent and the clinical considerations, since the absent or non- participating parent may later come forward to object to the treatment, demand that it stop, threaten to sue or

complain to a regulatory board, or request a copy of the minor's records.

If the therapist is confident that the judgment used was reasonable under the circumstances presented, the solution is often not very difficult. Some therapists who face such situations simply inform the parent that the treatment of the child was consented to by the other parent (and therefore lawful), and that the therapist is not of a mind to abandon the patient by a quick and clinically unwarranted termination. The threatened complaint or lawsuit usually does not materialize. In the event that they do materialize, the therapist will have malpractice insurance that provides coverage for, among other things, defending a lawsuit and defending a disciplinary matter (complaint to a regulatory board).

As to access to the child's records, therapists may be required by applicable law to permit access even to non-custodial parents under specified circumstances. It is vital for therapists to know their jurisdiction's laws and regulations in precise detail.

DETERMINING CUSTODY

In cases where a court has entered a custody or visitation order, ask for a copy of the order to determine the nature of the custody arrangement. In most jurisdictions, custody has two components: "legal custody" (who has the legal right to make decisions on behalf of the child relating to the child's health, education and welfare), and "physical custody" (with whom the child resides). When a court orders "joint legal custody," this usually means that the parents share the right and responsibility to make important decisions on behalf of their child. In other words, either parent may consent to the treatment of the child, unless the court has specified in the order that the consent of both parents is required.

The therapist may be uncomfortable interpreting the terms of the court order or determining whether or not the conditions in the court order have been satisfied. For instance, the court order might order joint legal custody but specify that the parties "consult" with one another prior to obtaining "medical care" for the child. What if one parent says that they have "consulted" with the other parent and that such other parent does not want the child to be in psychotherapy? Does "medical care" include counseling by an MFT? If in doubt, the therapist can consult with a local attorney, decline to treat, or request the consent of both parents.

EXERCISING DISCRETION

Suppose a parent seeks treatment for a child, and the therapist determines that the parent has been awarded visitation (but no physical custody) and joint legal custody (without a requirement for the consent of both). The parent seeking treatment for the child requests that the other parent not be informed of the treatment of the child. While the therapist may be permitted by law to treat the child with the consent of the parent who has joint legal custody, sound discretion may indicate otherwise. Suppose, however, that treatment of the child does begin. What might the therapist experience?

Perhaps the first words from the child will disclose drug use or vague allegations of abuse, neglect, or emotional harm by the custodial parent. What if the parent who brings the child to treatment wants to be better positioned in a custody battle and is intending to call the therapist as a witness and to subpoena the child's records in order to prevail in the litigation, or has unduly influenced the child in order to prompt a child abuse report by the treating therapist?

Such occurrences often take place. If the therapist initially requires notice to or the consent of the other parent before undertaking treatment, such hidden parental agendas may be brought to light and becoming enmeshed in the parents' litigation can perhaps be avoided.

AUTHORIZATIONS TO RELEASE INFORMATION AND MINOR CONSENT TO TREATMENT

When treating a child with parental consent, the general rule is that either parent can sign an authorization form to release confidential information about the child's treatment to a third party. A parent who has sole legal custody would ordinarily sign an authorization form on behalf of the minor. If there is joint legal custody, the general rule is that either parent can sign the authorization form, unless the court order has specified otherwise.

Some jurisdictions recognize a minor's right to control release of confidential information. If applicable law permits the minor to consent to the treatment without knowledge or consent of the parent, the minor must sign the authorization form. Depending on the law in question, that age can be as young as 12.

The ability of a minor to consent to treatment without parental consent can also be established by emancipation of the minor. Emancipation generally involves a legal proceeding. It can also result from parental consent or marriage.

When therapists agree to treat minors without knowledge or consent of a parent or guardian, therapists may need to attend to issues surrounding payment for services. For example, some laws expressly state that parents or guardians are not responsible for paying for services obtained without their consent or when they are not participating in services. Another issue that might emerge is related to the minor's use of insurance to pay for services since the policy holder will likely receive any explanations of benefits and, therefore, may become aware that services were provided to the minor.

Even in jurisdictions where minors can consent to services, some jurisdictions may require parental notice after a certain number of sessions, unless certain conditions are met. Therapists must be knowledgeable about the minor consent laws in their jurisdiction.

MINORS AND INFORMED CONSENT PAPERWORK

If you do a fair amount of work with children it may be appropriate to make your rules about access to the child's mental health record part of your informed consent document. Depending on applicable laws and the facts of a given situation, you may be entitled to deny a request for records if you believe that disclosure would be harmful to the child.

Don't forget to be clear about the identity of the client. If a custodial parent seeks "family" therapy with the child, the client is the family and the AAMFT Code of Ethics would require a written waiver from each individual in the client unit in order to disclose information outside the treatment context.

COMPLAINTS TO REGULATORY BOARDS

Regulatory boards receive a large number and significant percentage of complaints from people who are involved in custody or visitation disputes. A disgruntled parent may disagree with a therapist's findings or opinions, or may blame the therapist for a judge's adverse order. The more sophisticated regulatory boards, and those who investigate or make decisions regarding closing or pursuing a case, are usually aware that many of these complaints, especially those that allege that the therapist unlawfully treated the child without the consent of the complainant, are without merit.

Nevertheless, therapists who receive regulatory board requests for answers to specific questions, or those who receive calls from a state investigator wanting to discuss a complaint, would generally be well advised to consult with a lawyer knowledgeable in state administrative proceedings.

It is always the therapist's choice whether or not to undertake treatment of children or adults involved in litigation. It is also the therapist's choice whether or not to participate in the litigation by writing letters, reports, or treatment summaries, and risk antagonizing one or both parents.

Chapter 5: Confidentiality When Working with Couples and Families

When treating a couple or family, the therapist may decide to see one or more of the participants individually for one or more sessions, then return to seeing the couple or family in future sessions. Are the individual sessions to be viewed as part of the couple or family therapy? Are the individuals told that such is the case? Are they led to believe that the individual sessions are completely confidential, even as it relates to others participating in the therapy and even if the therapist believes that there is information that should be shared with the unit being treated in order for the couple or family work to be effective? It is important to be clear with participants in therapy and to let them know how you will handle such issues.

As systemic therapists, MFTs recognize that the "client" in a therapeutic relationship may be more than one person. Thus, it is commonly understood that the client may be a couple or a family. Ethical standards typically require that therapists disclose to "clients" **the nature of confidentiality** and **possible limitations on the clients' right to confidentiality**. If there are limitations, the disclosure is to be made as early as feasible in the professional relationship and may need to be made on more than one occasion as treatment progresses. Thus, prior to the commencement of couple or family therapy, it would be wise for therapists to inform the participants about the nature and extent of confidentiality as it relates to the services being sought.

Generally, the laws of confidentiality are intended to prevent unauthorized disclosures to third parties. If the identified client is a couple, most MFTs understand that before they release information about the couple, or any one of them, to a third party, they must obtain the written authorization of the client – that is, both persons who are participating in the couples work. If the therapist needs to see one or both of the participants for a few sessions individually, and then intends to return to working with both, it is important for the therapist to let the parties know that the couple remains the identified client, and that these sessions are to be considered a part of the process of couple therapy. This will probably confirm the belief of the participants.

What if the individual being seen now wanted the therapist to release only his individual records to a third party? The therapist would likely take the view that the signature of both or all parties would be needed, since these sessions, although with only one of the participants, were considered by all to be a part of the couples or family work. The therapist typically is not likely to have told the individuals involved that the therapeutic relationship with the couple or family was temporarily being terminated, or that the therapist was now beginning a new and separate professional relationship with the individual. The therapist's allegiance is to the client – that is, the couple or family.

Thus, when the parties are told that the individual sessions are a necessary part of the work with the couple or family, and that the therapist's primary allegiance and duty is to the client – that is, the couple or family, what is the individual to think about the confidentiality of communications with the therapist during those individual sessions? Isn't it reasonable for the client to expect that the communications will be confidential? What should the individual be told about the limitation to confidentiality? A "no secrets" policy (see below) is intended to answer those questions.

Not all communications from a client to a therapist are confidential. The law of confidentiality, from its very origins, was never intended to be absolute. If the client threatens imminent physical harm to self or others, most jurisdictions require or allow disclosure without the written authorization of the client. Child and elder abuse reporting laws require certain disclosures to be made. If the client utters words to his therapist in the waiting room and in the presence of others, there is generally no right to confidentiality with respect to that communication.

What the therapist is really telling the client by using a "no secrets" policy is that, while confidentiality is generally going to be protected and respected, it may become necessary for the therapist, in the reasonable exercise of clinical judgment, and in order to treat the client properly, to disclose certain information learned in the individual session to the actual client – that is, to the couple or the family (though not to a third party). The therapist will ultimately decide whether or not any disclosure needs to be made, what specific disclosures may be necessary, when the disclosure should be made, and by whom the disclosure should be made - all for the appropriate treatment of the couple or family. Such a disclosure should not be seen as an inappropriate or unlawful breach of the duty of confidentiality, but rather, as a necessary part of therapy.

It is important, again, to point out that such disclosures are not going to be made, if they are made at all, to a third party, but rather, to the client or client unit (the couple or family). The disclosures, if any, will be made in the best interests of the client and for treatment purposes, and for no other purpose. With the signature of all of the participants acknowledging the policy, the clients have been informed of both the nature of confidentiality and the possible limitation upon confidentiality as it pertains to couple or family work. They have also given the therapist their written permission to make the disclosures that are described in the policy.

The written permission obtained in this instance is not permission sought immediately prior to a desired disclosure, but rather, permission gained prior to the commencement of therapy and, in essence, as a precondition to embarking upon a course of couple or family therapy.

"No Secrets" Policy For Couple or Family Treatment

NOTE: This sample "no secrets" policy is intended to help therapists anticipate certain problems that may occur when providing therapy to couples or families. If any of the statements made in this sample policy do not accurately reflect your views or your method of practice, you should not include them in any policy that you may choose to use. The title of the form could be something other than a "No Secrets Policy", perhaps "Limitation on Confidentiality when Providing Therapy to Couples or Families." This sample is provided solely for information and educational purposes and should not be considered to be legal advice. Therapists are advised to consult with a local attorney to ensure that any policies, forms, etc., used in practice are consistent with all applicable laws.

This statement of policy is intended to inform you, the participants in therapy, that when I agree to treat a couple or a family, I consider that couple or family (the treatment unit) to be the client. For instance, if there is a request for the treatment records of the couple or the family, I will seek the authorization of all members of the treatment unit before I release confidential information to third parties. Also, if my records are subpoenaed, I will assert the psychotherapist-patient privilege on behalf of the client (treatment unit).

During the course of my work with a couple or a family, I may see a smaller part of the treatment unit (e.g., an individual or two siblings) for one or more sessions. These sessions should be seen by you as a part of the work that I am doing with the family or the couple, unless otherwise indicated. If you are involved in one or more of such sessions with me, please understand that generally these sessions are confidential in the sense that I will not release any confidential information to a third party unless I am required by law to do so, or unless I have your written authorization. In fact, since those sessions can and should be considered a part of the treatment of the couple or family, I would also seek the authorization of the other individuals in the treatment unit before releasing confidential information to a third party.

However, I may need to share information learned in an individual session (or a session with only a portion of the treatment unit being present) with the entire treatment unit – that is, the family or the couple, if I am

effectively to serve the unit being treated. I will use my best judgment as to whether, when, and to what extent I will make disclosures to the treatment unit, and I will also, if appropriate, first give the individual or the smaller part of the treatment unit being seen the opportunity to make the disclosure. Thus, if you feel it necessary to talk about matters that you absolutely want to be shared with no one, you might want to consult with an individual therapist who can treat you individually.

This "no secrets" policy is intended to allow me to continue to treat the couple or family by preventing, to the extent possible, a conflict of interest from arising when an individual's interests may not be consistent with the interests of the unit being treated. For instance, information learned in the course of an individual session may be relevant or even essential to the proper treatment of the couple or the family. If I am not free to exercise my clinical judgment regarding the need to bring this information to the family or the couple during their therapy, I might be placed in a situation where I will have to terminate treatment of the couple or the family. This policy is intended to prevent the need for such a termination.

By signing below, you, as members of the couple/family or other unit receiving treatment, acknowledge that each of you has read this policy, that you understand it, that you have had an opportunity to discuss its contents with me as your therapist, and that you undertake couple/family therapy in agreement with this policy.

ated: _____   Signature: _____

Dated: _____   Signature: _____

Dated: _____   Signature: _____

Use additional date and signature lines as is necessary. If someone is signing in a representative apacity, such as a parent or a court-appointed guardian or conservator, such capacity should be tated and the person being represented should be specified.)

Chapter 6: Termination of Treatment – Legal and Ethical Considerations

There are a variety of considerations and potential problems connected with termination of treatment. If the process of termination is not properly carried out, the attempt to end therapy can constitute abandonment of the client, which may result in a complaint to the regulatory board or a civil action for damages. Additionally, a failure to pay attention to the issue of termination may result in a therapist being held liable for harm to the client, even though the therapist was under the impression that the therapist-client relationship had ended.

Generally, clients have the right to terminate treatment at any time and for any reason. Therapists commonly terminate treatment a) when the course of treatment has come to a natural end because of the improvement of the client, b) when the client is no longer able to pay for treatment pursuant to the original agreement, c) when the therapist has determined that the client's problem is beyond the therapist's scope of competence, d) when the therapist determines that the client is not benefiting from the treatment, e) when the therapist is unable or unwilling, for appropriate reasons, to continue to provide care, or f) when the treating therapist leaves his or her employment, either voluntarily or involuntarily.

UNWILLING OR UNABLE TO CONTINUE TO PROVIDE CARE

There are many situations that may justify or require termination by the therapist under this category. Perhaps the client is not attending sessions regularly or canceling sessions to such a degree that the therapist believes adequate treatment is compromised, and the client's problem cannot be resolved, or may even be worsened, by such pattern of attendance. Perhaps a client is not willing to take the therapist's referrals to a physician for a physical examination or evaluation for medication, or to others for recommended diagnosis or treatment. Perhaps a conflict arises that, in the opinion of the therapist, requires a termination.

Additionally, therapists may retire, move, or be forced to suspend, close or limit their practices due to illness or other reasons. Clients should be informed of the impending termination well in advance of a planned retirement, and with as much prior notice as circumstances permit or clinical considerations dictate in other cases. Wherever possible, the termination should be discussed with the client and provisions should be made for the continued care of the client.

DISCHARGE FROM EMPLOYMENT

When a therapist leaves an employed position, either voluntarily or involuntarily, what communications should occur with the client? Therapists who are discharged with little prior notice express concerns about the client, and often want to contact the client in an effort to have the client follow them to their new location, or to explain why the therapist will not be present at the next session. This is usually not a good idea. The therapist is generally best served by promptly contacting the employer (confirmed in writing) to express concerns about the client because of the sudden termination.

The therapist can request that the employer inform the client of the client's options – that is, to remain at the agency and see another therapist, to leave the agency and be referred elsewhere or to continue to see the departing therapist at the therapist's new location, unless the terms of the therapist's employment prohibit it. The therapist should remind the employer of the importance of continuity of care and the duty to act in the client's best interests. The therapist can also let the employer know, if appropriate, that the employer bears responsibility for any client harm due to the sudden and inappropriate termination of the therapist and the failure to fully inform the client of his or her options.

If the termination takes place over a period of time, as when the therapist gives notice that she is leaving, the therapist can inform the client of the options. Often, the employer will protest and will not want the client to follow the departing therapist, or even be informed of the options available. Again, all parties have a duty to act in the client's best interests. Sometimes, the employer tries to enforce a written agreement where the therapist has either promised not to take employer clients to the new location, or where the therapist has agreed to pay money to the employer for doing so. Therapists should seek consultation with a local attorney to determine the enforceability of such clauses. In addition, therapists who are asked to sign employment agreements or contracts are well advised to seek legal counsel prior to entering into such agreements or contracts.

DISCLOSURE STATEMENTS AND TERMINATION

Many therapists use some form of disclosure statement, either because it is legally required or because the therapist finds it useful in establishing the ground rules for the commencement of a professional relationship. Typically included in these statements are such matters as the therapists' treatment philosophy or approach to therapy, their credentials, their hours of availability, what to do in cases of an emergency, the fee to be charged for services and information about confidentiality and the exceptions thereto. The issue of termination can also be addressed in the disclosure statement, which may prove helpful to the therapist at the time of termination.

The disclosure statement can explain that the client has the right to terminate at any time and for any reason. The therapist may want to state a preference that if the client desires to terminate the relationship, the client should discuss termination with the therapist in advance so that there can be proper closure, including referrals where appropriate, and so that any misunderstandings may be resolved. While the client may ultimately choose to ignore this stated preference, it is quite reasonable and professional to include at the inception of therapy.

It may also prove useful to inform the client, in the statement, that if the client is unable to continue to pay the agreed upon fee, the client should speak with the therapist promptly so that the therapist can decide whether or not treatment will continue (perhaps the therapist will lower the fee or work pro bono for a period of time), or whether treatment will be terminated and a referral made.

Perhaps most helpful, especially in difficult cases, is for the disclosure statement to inform the client that the therapist is ethically bound to terminate therapy when it is reasonably clear that the client is not benefiting from the therapy. Many therapists have experienced the difficult client who may not be willing to let go of the relationship. Letting the client know, early in the process, of one's ethical duties in this regard may ease the termination process with such clients.

PROCESS OF TERMINATION

Therapists who would get in trouble are those who, with little or no prior discussion with the client, terminate treatment, perhaps by writing a letter, speaking on the telephone or leaving a message. Ethical practice usually demands more. Terminations initiated by the therapist should generally be the result of a process where the client is given time to meet with the therapist to discuss the reasons for the termination, and where transition to other care, if appropriate or necessary, is discussed. In general, the longer the therapeutic relationship has been in effect, the longer the period of time needed for the termination process.

Although sessions held for the purpose of discussing termination issues are a part of the therapy process and are properly billed for, therapists may want to consider waiving some or all of the fee in order to lessen the burden on the client. With respect to the issue of transition to other care, therapists must not only be prepared to make thoughtful referrals, but must also think about making a reasonable effort to follow through with the client to determine whether or not the client is receiving the recommended care.

In some cases, a client may not show up for one or more sessions and may not respond to inquiries by the therapist. Failure to clarify the status of the therapist-client relationship could result in problems for the therapist, since the client may later claim that there was never a termination, just a lull in the treatment. When the client later calls in crisis, it may be difficult for the therapist to maintain that there had been a termination and that he or she is not accepting "new" clients. If the therapist fails to treat the client when he or she re-presents, this could lead to a charge of abandonment – at the time that the client claims to be most in need.

Termination by the therapist is most difficult with clients who are in serious emotional distress, including those who are suicidal or those who feign suicide. The client will often be reluctant to end the relationship even though a termination may, in the opinion of the therapist, be in the best interests of the client. In such situations (and others), it is useful to obtain one or more clinical consultations. A termination in these circumstances may require the therapist to warn others of the client's suicidal threats. Many jurisdictions usually either allow or require disclosure when the client is in such mental or emotional condition as to be a danger to self and disclosure is necessary to avert such danger. Therapists should adhere to any applicable laws, including any provisions that discuss how the therapist should proceed (e.g. should a report be made to a particular entity, is hospitalization of the client an option).

WHO IS THE CLIENT?

Therapists sometimes have trouble identifying the client. Perhaps the original identified client was a couple, but it later turned into individual therapy when one of the participants dropped out of therapy. Perhaps the therapist was working with an individual, but the therapy later turned into couple or family therapy.

While it is sometimes difficult to pigeonhole treatment into one category or another, therapists should pay attention to the question of client identity so that they can be clear – both to the participants directly and in the records – when the therapist-client relationship changes. It may be necessary or advisable to let one or more of the participants know that there has been a termination of a prior relationship, and that, for the future, a different relationship exists.

DUAL RELATIONSHIPS AND TERMINATION

Generally speaking, therapists are well advised to avoid dual or multiple relationships with clients both during the therapist-client relationship and following a termination. However, some jurisdictions do not prohibit even a sexual relationship between a therapist and a former client following the termination of the therapeutic relationship. Many laws on this issue specify an amount of time that must pass after the termination of the relationship before any type of sexual relationship could be contemplated. Some laws may also include language indicating that terminating a therapist-client relation-ship for the sole purpose of entering into a sexual relationship with the client would constitute unprofessional conduct. A therapist

who is going to engage in any kind of post-therapy relationship with a former client must be certain that the termination process was "clean," uncontaminated, and well documented, and that the therapist is in compliance with all applicable laws and ethical mandates. Therapists must be knowledgeable about their jurisdictions' laws and any ethical mandates to which they are held; it's possible that ethical mandates may be stricter (e.g. prohibit sexual relationships with former clients, regardless of the amount of time that has passed), or vice versa. At the time of publication, the AAMFT Code of Ethics prohibits sexual intimacy with current and former clients, as well as with known members of the client's family system.

With respect to nonsexual relationships with former clients, such as friendship or business relationships, therapists must be careful that enough time has passed from the date of termination such that the risks of exploitation and impairment of judgment have been eliminated. While there is not a specific amount of time that must pass, the risks associated with such relationships may decrease with a greater amount of time passing. However, therapists should be aware that regardless of the amount of time that has passed, there may be some level of risk that cannot be eliminated in these situations.

A major problem with any kind of post-therapy relationship is that the therapist is always at risk for a charge that the therapist improperly foreclosed the client's right to future care in order to satisfy the therapist's current needs (some may argue that this would constitute client exploitation).

TERMINATION LETTERS

The termination process should be well documented in the treatment records, regardless of who initiates the termination. When the process goes smoothly, there may be no need to confirm the termination by letter. When the termination process is more volatile, it is more likely that the therapist may want to send a letter to confirm the termination and the reasons for it, including who initiated the termination. In more ambiguous situations, where, for example, a client simply doesn't show up for appointments, the therapist may want first to reach out to the client in an effort to clarify the client's intentions. This can usually be done by telephone and confirmed thereafter in writing.

Before writing to a client, the therapist must have permission from the client to send letters to the client at a particular address. The letter must be carefully drafted and must be an accurate reflection of what has occurred. It should be consistent with the records and, to the extent possible, not be inflammatory. If the client later decides to take action against the therapist, the therapist must be able to defend the appropriateness of each statement in the letter. Before sending such a letter, therapists would be wise to consult with a respected colleague and with legal counsel.

While termination letters may be appropriate, some form of personal communication with documentation of the conversation in the records may be less taxing. Following the personal communication (often by telephone), it is usually easier to write a letter confirming the essence of the conversation, including the reasons for the termination. Sometimes a letter will simply confirm the fact that, despite several attempts by the therapist, the client fails to respond or refuses to discuss the issue.

If the termination involves a referral of the client to a different therapist, consider confirming the referral(s) in writing, and making a statement of a specific window of availability to permit the client to make the transfer. "Please feel free to contact me at any time for the next two weeks," may help avoid a complaint for abandonment.

Chapter 7: Client Suicide

When the unthinkable happens, self-care is important. Consulting with a colleague and time to reflect before being drawn into the inevitable aftermath of a client suicide are essential.

Suppose you receive a call from a police officer reporting the death of your client and wanting to talk with you as part of an investigation. Or a family member calls you to report that your client committed suicide last night and the family needs a copy of the file for the inquest.

Before you take any steps, even if you suspect that the client's death may not have been a suicide, take a moment to locate the client file and call your malpractice carrier. **You are not admitting liability or subjecting yourself to adverse action.** The insurance company will be able to advise you of appropriate next steps that will help you and the insurance company if there should ever be a claim made against you in the future.

Consulting with your professional liability carrier will give you access to information that will help you respond appropriately. For example, if there is no exception to the rules governing confidentiality, you may need to maintain confidentiality or invoke any applicable privilege until it is waived by an appropriate individual (e.g. administrator of client's estate, executor of client's estate).

Finally, accurate documentation of therapists' comprehensive assessment of suicide risk in clients helps reduce liability. Although errors of judgment (failure to *accurately* assess suicide potential) may be inevitable, errors of omission (failure to *adequately* assess suicide potential) are preventable. Therapists should be aware of all applicable laws in their jurisdictions and should be knowledgeable about the standard of care when assessing suicide risk. Therapists may benefit from seeking opportunities to enhance their suicide assessment and intervention skills (in fact, some jurisdictions require a certain amount of continuing education in suicide prevention).

PART III:
THE THERAPIST
AND THE COURT

Chapter 1: Working with Clients Involved in Court Proceedings

A frequent issue in ethics and legal consultations involves confidentiality and conflict of interest for members who work with clients who are involved in court proceedings.

While MFTs may more regularly find themselves working with clients involved in family court proceedings (e.g. divorce, custody), the types of court proceedings in which clients may become involved include criminal court matters, employment litigation, personal injury cases, and more. Regardless of the type of court proceedings in question, therapists are well advised to attend to issues surrounding confidentiality, dual roles, and conflicts of interest, just to name a few. It is critical when undertaking therapy with clients involved in court proceedings that everyone understand what the object of the therapy is, whether and to whom the therapist is required to report about the therapy, and what the limits of confidentiality are when clients participate because they are required to do so. A special or limited-purpose informed consent document may be appropriate in these circumstances.

To examine these issues, imagine a therapist who has been working with a mother who is going to court to seek a modification of the parties' custody agreement. The therapist has only treated the mother; the therapist has never met the father or minor children. The mother asks the therapist to write a letter in support of the mother's request to modify the custody agreement.

The moment the therapist agrees to write a letter, or testify, or talk to a lawyer, the therapist ceases to be a therapist and becomes an advocate. A letter that offers an opinion on whether or not custody should be modified is clearly a forensic evaluation and the responsibility of an expert.

As difficult as it may be, the therapist must not be a helper in this situation. In addition to the ethical considerations involving dual roles and conflicts of interest, the reality is that if the decision in the custody proceeding goes against the mother or if the mother feels that the therapist's involvement in the litigation negatively impacted her in any way, it's possible that the therapeutic relationship will be adversely affected.

Another possible scenario that could arise is one where the client or the client's lawyer asks the therapist to participate in a case by some other means (e.g. testifying, completing an affidavit). Again, when this occurs the lawyer is almost always looking for an expert opinion. To a lawyer or court, "expert" means someone who is qualified to give opinions at trial. It doesn't mean superstar or genius, but merely a person whose background and experience impresses a court enough to allow an opinion about something. Fact or "lay" witnesses testify about what they have seen, heard, or felt.

You may feel compelled to testify for your own current or past client, and the lawyer may try to ease you into it by starting out with simple questions about the course of your treatment, and then asking for an opinion. Don't do it. There is a substantial conflict of interest between treating and expert roles.

Attorneys often refer their clients for treatment, assuming the therapist will testify if needed. Beware of lawyers (and clients) who would place you in an unethical position. Once a person is your client, you must act in the client's interest. You cannot be an expert and objective, even if you believe you can. When a lawyer sends a client for treatment, make it clear to the attorney and the client that you will not be available for expert testimony. Both you and the client should be aware that if the referral has anything to do with litigation, the treatment will also be compromised to some degree by the possibility that the other side could subpoena the records.

The function of therapist and advocate is clearly a dual relationship. A treatment relationship clearly creates a professional and ethical obligation to act in the best interests of the client.

The purpose and goals of the treating therapist are different from those of the expert witness. The clinician has fiduciary and ethical obligations to the client which demand that the client's interests be placed first.

Therapists should be knowledgeable about their jurisdiction's laws and regulations applicable to these scenarios, as well as ethical mandates. Therapists who regularly work with clients involved in court proceedings would benefit from being knowledgeable about the legal systems in which their clients are involved (e.g. family courts, criminal courts).

Chapter 2: The Subpoena

Questions about subpoenas frequently top the list of calls and e-mails to AAMFT's legal/ethics consultation service.

A subpoena taped to your office door, handed to you by a process server or delivered in the mail, is annoying at best and alarming at worst. It is the first step in a pageant in which you have no choice but to participate. It can be helpful to prepare ahead of time and know what steps to take and when to take them.

Some MFTs attempt to avoid being subpoenaed into court by including provisions in an informed consent document advising the client that the therapist will not participate in litigation. While this type of notice to a client may have some limiting effect, whether or not it is enforceable has yet to be tested. Further, it is often the opposing side that issues the subpoena.

SUBPOENAS IN GENERAL

An attorney issues a subpoena so that the client's case can be proved by introducing documents or testimony into evidence. A subpoena is a process of the courts, not of the parties. Although a subpoena may be issued by an attorney, it is a mandate of the court, issued for the court.

A subpoena is an order of a sort. The Latin root translates as "under penalty." The recipient of a subpoena is commanded to appear "under penalty" of contempt. Failure to show up and testify, either at deposition or at trial, and/or to produce documents (subpoena duces tecum—"bring with you") can result in an order of contempt against the therapist,

meaning fines, payment of attorneys' fees, and potentially jail time.

Do not let the word "order" in a subpoena confuse you, or the lawyer issuing the subpoena intimidate you. A subpoena is not the type of court order that permits a client's confidentiality to be breached. Therapists are trained to preserve confidentiality. A therapist's first response to a subpoena should be to resist, thereby protecting the client. But the resistance needs to be well thought out and properly executed in order to avoid a finding of contempt.

SPECIFIC STEPS IN RESPONDING TO A SUBPOENA

The specific steps that a therapist will need to take to appropriately respond to a subpoena will vary based on the facts of the situation at hand and applicable laws. Therapists are advised to consult with a local attorney whenever they receive a subpoena. Therapists are also advised to contact their professional liability insurer for assistance in responding to the subpoena. The therapist's professional liability coverage may provide payment for legal fees and expenses related to subpoenas.

Generally speaking, the first step after receiving a subpoena is to review the subpoena and all accompanying documents. By doing so you should be able to identify the names of the parties, the date, time and place you will need to appear and/or bring records, the name of the lawyer who issued the subpoena, and the location and type of court in which the lawsuit is taking place.

When you have gleaned the basic information from the subpoena and identified which of your clients is involved, determine whether the attorney issuing the subpoena is the attorney for your client or the attorney for the party opposing your client. The identity of the subpoena issuer is significant in regard to protecting your client's confidentiality, and because of privilege that you may be able to invoke on your client's behalf. This is important not only for your client, but also for you, since you could be liable to your client for breaching confidentiality and subject to discipline by your regulatory board for unethical or unprofessional conduct.

If the attorney issuing the subpoena represents your client, you could conclude that the client has waived any applicable "psychotherapist-client" privilege and that you are not breaching your duty to the client by turning over the requested documents or testifying at a deposition or at trial. However, many codes of ethics and most jurisdictions' laws governing confidentiality require that a waiver be in writing.

After identifying the parties involved and the attorney who issued the subpoena, determining the validity of the subpoena is advisable. A subpoena could be found to be invalid for various reasons, including technical defects with the subpoena, defective service of the subpoena, or issues related to whether the therapist is subject to the jurisdiction in which the litigation is pending (e.g. therapist is located in a different jurisdiction than where the litigation is pending). Some defects are relatively easy to cure, so just because it may be possible to argue that a subpoena is invalid doesn't mean that such arguments will

be made. Consultation with a local attorney is advisable if you have questions about the validity of a subpoena.

Looking to the client or client unit to determine whether all necessary parties are waiving confidentiality and any applicable privilege is one option when a therapist receives a subpoena. Although some recommend contacting the client, others may not. If the client is still in treatment, contacting the client involves the therapist in the client's life outside of therapy. It may be the case that the client doesn't know the lawyers' legal strategy, and the subpoena will be a surprise. The therapist would effectively be taking their cue from the client. In some situations, therapists may wish to speak to the client's attorney about whether information should be disclosed pursuant to a subpoena. Before doing so, however, therapists must first obtain the client's written consent to do so. Additionally, therapists are advised to remember that the client's attorney does not represent the therapist and therapists may need to seek independent legal counsel to aid them in responding to a subpoena.

If the client does not waive confidentiality and any applicable privilege, the client's attorney may be helpful in filing a motion to quash subpoena or other appropriate motions that could relieve the therapist from the subpoena. If the client does not have an attorney or the client's attorney is unable or unwilling to file appropriate motions, the therapist may need to obtain their own legal counsel for specific advice on how to proceed. Similarly, if the therapist is unable to reach the client to discuss the subpoena, the therapist may need to invoke privilege on behalf of the client or ient unit. In such situations, consultation with local attorney is advisable.

epending on applicable laws, in some tuations a written objection, citing the rivileged nature of the information sought, ɔ the attorney who issued the subpoena may e appropriate. In any communication with the suing attorney, the therapist would typically ot be able to acknowledge the therapist lient relationship without the client's written ɔnsent. Therapists might need to use anguage indicating that the therapist can either confirm nor deny that a therapist-client elationship exists.

ome attorneys will acknowledge the privilege nd volunteer to secure the appropriate eleases. Others will threaten contempt of ourt for ignoring the subpoena. Do not be ntimidated by threats or rants. Most jurisdic- ions recognize a mental health professional/ lient privilege in one way or another. Also eep in mind that you are within your rights to efuse to speak to the attorney and to request hat all communication be in writing.

he absence of a release or waiver of privilege y the client is more significant for the herapist who has been treating a couple ɔr family. The client unit (couple, family or roup) is typically seen as the holder of the rivilege and all participants must waive the rivilege before the therapist can lawfully and thically produce documents or give testimony bout any participant in the couple, family or roup. Without that waiver, law and ethics equire an order, signed by a judge, directing he therapist by name to produce testimony ɔr documents.

Such an order protects the therapist in two areas. First, all licensing statutes require professional conduct and ethical practice on the part of license holders.

Those same licensing statutes identify breach of client confidentiality as an instance of unprofessional conduct or unethical practice. Therefore, a therapist who complies with a subpoena without releases or waivers from all clients puts the license at risk for denial, revocation or suspension. Second, a therapist who breaches a client's confidentiality without the court ordering the disclosure is at risk for an allegation of malpractice. The therapist owes a duty of confidentiality to the client. A therapist who provides testimony or produces documents without a waiver from the client or a court order, breaches that duty and may be liable for any damage resulting from that breach of duty.

SUBPOENA CHECKLIST:

❏ Where are you required to appear?

❏ Are you required to bring documents with you?

❏ When are you required to appear?

Depending on applicable laws, if you have received inadequate notice, this could be grounds for quashing a subpoena. In some situations, the issuing attorney may be able to reschedule deposition or production of record dates. Consultation with a local attorney is advised in these situations.

❏ Does the subpoena contain a check for witness fees and expenses?

When therapists are subpoenaed to appear at a deposition or hearing, they may be able to request a witness fee in the amount of the number of hours the hearing or deposition is expected to last multiplied by the therapist's hourly fee. This does not guarantee that the therapist will receive payment, and the therapist cannot condition the therapist's appearance on being paid. The amount that a therapist might be entitled to may depend on the type of witness the therapist is being called as (e.g. expert vs. fact), local court rules, and applicable law. (As a reminder, treating therapists who act as expert witnesses may put themselves in jeopardy of violating applicable laws and ethical mandates to avoid dual roles and conflicts of interest.)

❏ Does the subpoena contain a release signed by your client authorizing you to testify and/ or produce documents?

Chapter 3: Understanding Privilege

Many mental health practitioners are unclear about the difference between confidentiality and privilege. The distinction is important, and understanding the difference between the two concepts is essential to an understanding of how to respond to a subpoena.

Simply put, confidentiality is a general restriction (by law and by ethical standards) on the volunteering of information pertaining to your client, while privilege involves the right to withhold testimony or records in a legal proceeding. (For a discussion on selected issues in confidentiality, you can refer back to Chapter 1 in Section II of this book.) It is important for mental health practitioners to know whether or not they are covered by a psychotherapist-patient privilege (the privilege may be called something else), and whether or not the privilege applies in both civil and criminal cases. This chapter assumes that the reader is fully covered by the privilege.

The general rule is that no person has a right to refuse to testify in a legal proceeding if properly subpoenaed. Likewise, the general rule is that documents/records may be obtained in a legal proceeding if a lawful subpoena is issued, and no person can refuse to produce such evidence.

There are exceptions to these general rules based on specific well-recognized and confidential relationships. The primary privileges recognized by most jurisdictions are the attorney-client, physician-patient, clergy-penitent, psychotherapist-client, and husband-wife privileges. The patient, client, penitent or spouse can generally prevent the therapist, attorney, spouse or clergyperson from disclosing information or records by claiming, asserting, or invoking the privilege.

Legislatures have decided that there is a greater societal benefit in excluding this kind of evidence in legal proceedings than there is in allowing the court to have the benefit of the evidence, even though the information may be relevant to the issues involved. The greater public benefit in excluding the testimony is that people will be encouraged to communicate fully and openly with their therapists (and others covered by a privilege) so that they can get the help that they need without the fear that their confidential communications or records will later be revealed in a legal proceeding.

Your treatment of your client is a confidential matter. Without your client's authorization to disclose that treatment, you must protect client confidentiality and invoke the therapist/client privilege. However, therapists must understand that the privilege typically belongs to the client. If the client waives it, you must disclose whatever information the client authorizes you to disclose. With the signed waiver in your file, the client cannot later complain that you breached your duty of maintaining client confidentiality.

WAIVER OF PRIVILEGE BY OPERATION OF LAW AND PROTECTIVE ORDERS

Many clients do not realize that if they are suing for mental or emotional distress, their mental state may be an issue in the lawsuit, and the privilege may have been waived giving the opposition access to all of their records and to the therapist's testimony. However, as the therapist invoking the client's privilege, you need not rely on an attorney involved in the litigation telling you that this is the case.

Some jurisdictions have a procedure whereby the attorney seeking the records gives notice to the client's attorney that a subpoena will be served on the therapist, and, unless the client's attorney objects, any privilege will be considered waived. This type of proceeding can be confusing to a therapist who receives a copy of a subpoena along with a notice that the subpoena will be served in 30 days.

If the client does not object, the therapist receives the actual, signed subpoena, but there is still no release attached. Since most licensing statutes require that a client's waiver of confidentiality be in writing, the therapist is still at some risk for releasing information, even though the client did not object. In these situations, if the therapist does not have a written waiver demonstrating that all necessary parties have waived the privilege, the therapist should consider asking the court for a protective order, especially if the records are those of a client unit in treatment (e.g., a couple or a family) and only one member of that unit is involved in litigation. A protective order is a court order of the type that protects the therapist who discloses confidential information without a written waiver from the client.

In this situation, your professional liability insurer may provide payment for legal representation for you to avoid a future claim that you breached the client's confidentiality.

DETERMINING PRIVILEGE

Perhaps you are treating a person under the age of eighteen. In some jurisdictions, the holder of the privilege is the minor (since the minor is the client), even where the minor is a very young child. If records were subpoenaed in one of those jurisdictions, the therapist would assert the privilege on behalf of the child and not release the records unless ordered by the court or unless authorized by the child's attorney or some other person appointed by the court to represent the interests of the child in the legal proceeding. While parents are the natural guardians of their children and generally exercise legal control of them, when it comes to privilege, the parents may not hold the privilege.

It is important to know who the client is because you may need to assert privilege on his/her/their behalf. Thus, a couple or an entire family might well be the holder of the privilege, and a waiver may not be fully effective unless all parties in the unit waive the privilege. The general rule is that if persons are in therapy to further the interests of a particular client (or each other) in the consultation or the treatment, the privilege is not waived by the presence of those other persons. This general rule should protect the privilege in cases involving group therapy, couples therapy, or family therapy. With respect to a deceased client, the privilege generally survives the death of the client and the personal representative of the deceased would usually be a holder of the privilege.

Each case is different and laws vary across jurisdictions. You should obtain a legal consultation whenever you are uncertain about how to proceed. If you make a mistake in this area of practice, it is usually better if you make a mistake by withholding production of the records than if you make a mistake by releasing the records. Remember, your first instinct when served with a subpoena for records should be to resist. If you are covered by the psychotherapist-patient privilege, your duty is to assert the privilege and protect the client's privacy until properly instructed otherwise by your client or the court.